W9-CDG-802

🕮 READERS

Level 3

Level 4

A Note to Parents

DK READERS is a compelling program for beginning readers, designed in conjunction with leading literacy experts, including Dr. Linda Gambrell, Distinguished Professor of Education at Clemson University. Dr. Gambrell has served as President of the National Reading Conference, the College Reading Association, and the International Reading Association.

Beautiful illustrations and superb full-color photographs combine with engaging, easy-to-read stories to offer a fresh approach to each subject in the series. Each DK READER is guaranteed to capture a child's interest while developing his or her reading skills, general knowledge, and love of reading.

The five levels of DK READERS are aimed at different reading abilities, enabling you to choose the books that are exactly right for your child:

Pre-level 1: Learning to read
Level 1: Beginning to read
Level 2: Beginning to read alone
Level 3: Reading alone
Level 4: Proficient readers

The "normal" age at which a child begins to read can be anywhere from three to eight years old. Adult participation through the lower levels is very helpful for providing encouragement, discussing storylines, and sounding out unfamiliar words.

No matter which level you select, you can be sure that you are helping your child learn to read, then read to learn!

LONDON, NEW YORK, MUNICH,
MELBOURNE, and DELHI

Editorial Assistant Ruth Amos
Design Assistant Satvir Sihota
Jacket Designers Liam Drane,
Satvir Sihota
Senior Editor Victoria Taylor
Pre-Production Producer Siu Yin Chan
Producer Louise Daly
Reading Consultant Dr. Linda Gambrell
Design Manager Nathan Martin
Publishing Manager Julie Ferris
Art Director Ron Stobbart
Publishing Director Simon Beecroft

First published in the United States in 2013
by DK Publishing
375 Hudson Street
New York, New York 10014
10 9 8 7 6 5 4 3 2 1

DK books are available at special discounts when
purchased in bulk for sales promotions, premiums,
fund-raising, or educational use.
For details, contact:
DK Publishing Special Markets
375 Hudson Street
New York, New York 10014
SpecialSales@dk.com

A catalog record for this book is available
from the Library of Congress.

ISBN: 978-1-4654-0865-5 (Paperback)
ISBN: 978-1-4654-0866-2 (Hardcover)

Printed and bound by L.Rex, China
Color reproduction by Altaimage in the UK

Discover more at

www.dk.com

Contents

DK READERS

READING 3 ALONE

LEGO LEGENDS OF CHIMA

THE RACE FOR CHI

WRITTEN BY RUTH AMOS

Greetings brave adventurer!

This is the Legend of Chima. Chima is a land of great beauty and terrifying battles. It was once a peaceful paradise, but now the calm has been destroyed. Epic fights have broken out between the animal tribes who live here.

The animals are fighting for CHI. CHI is a powerful natural element, and the life force of this kingdom. It is a form of pure energy, giving awesome powers and enormous strength to those animals who learn how to wield it.

Where does CHI come from?

Mount Cavora is the biggest of Chima's mysterious mountains, floating up in the sky above the land. CHI flows as a liquid down Mount Cavora's many waterfalls and then down through Chima's rivers. Finally it flows into the Sacred Pool of CHI in the Lion Temple. Here it becomes solid blue orbs of CHI.

The Lions are the sworn guardians of the CHI, and are responsible for collecting CHI from the Sacred Pool. They distribute about 50 pieces of CHI to each animal tribe every month, at the huge "CHI Day" celebrations.

A piece of CHI

Mount Cavora floats in the sky.

The power of CHI

The Legend Beasts lived thousands of years ago. They walked on four legs just like normal animals. But one day some of them drank CHI from the river. These animals began to walk on two legs and evolved into the new species that live here today.

Armor holds CHI.

The animals use CHI to fuel their weapons, vehicles, and themselves. The animals wear special chest plates, that can hold the CHI. The CHI gives the animals an incredible power boost, and even improves their fighting skills!

The animals gain great strength when they insert the CHI into their armor.

Chest plate

Balancing act

Three of Chima's most important tribes are the Crocodiles, the Ravens, and the Wolves. They are greedy and plot to take all of the precious CHI for themselves. The CHI that powers their weapons glows red, to show that they have bad intentions.

The CHI glows red in the naughty Crocodiles' weapons.

The blue CHI core strengthens this Lion sword.

However, the Lion and the Eagle Tribes aim to share the CHI equally with everybody. Their CHI-powered weapons glow blue, to show their good intentions.

It is very important that the CHI is shared equally—if some tribes have more than others, then its energy will be unbalanced. There will be terrible consequences for all of Chima!

Animals stand at the back of their Speedorz.

Silver-tipped spear

Sleek design for super speed

Eagle Tribe symbols decorate the Speedor.

Competition day dawns

Today is a Speedor Tournament day! This is an epic race at Chima's Grand Arena. The animals ride on Speedorz, which are powerful chariots. The races test the riders' strength, agility, and daring.

Today the race is an obstacle course. On your mark! The fastest animal will win a glorious prize—an orb of rare Golden CHI. Golden CHI has never-ending power. The energy in normal blue-colored CHI only lasts for a few weeks.

Speedor Wheel
The big Speedor Wheel is made from a TribeStone. The stones fell from Mount Cavora and are thousands of years old.

The race begins

And they're off! The animals zoom away on their Speedorz through the obstacle course. The crowds cheer them on wildly. The competitors must have nerves of steel as they jump through sizzling rings of fire. They also dodge toppling boulders and collapsing caves!

Burning ring of fire

Equila from the Eagle Tribe is knocking down the raven targets, while Winzar of the Wolf Tribe drives straight through an ancient Ice Tower, smashing it to smithereens! Every animal is desperate to win the race and earn the rare Golden CHI for their tribe.

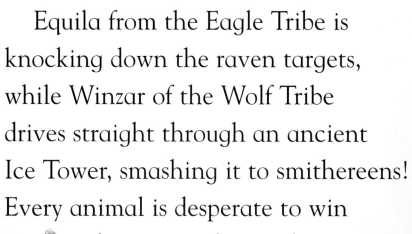

Red disk

The competitors must hit the colored disks to knock down the raven targets.

Crocodile carnage

As the competitors approach the finish line, King Crominus of the Crocodile Tribe is racing ahead, in the lead. But then disaster strikes! A huge pile of falling boulders throws him off balance and he crashes!

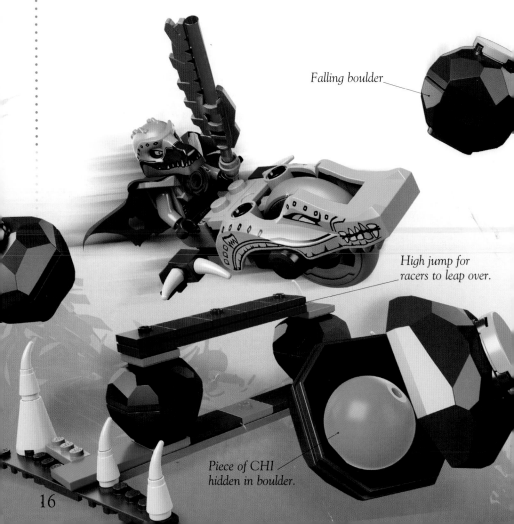

Falling boulder

High jump for racers to leap over.

Piece of CHI hidden in boulder.

Lennox
of the Lion Tribe
summons all his energy
and zooms under the ancient jungle
gates. He wins! Victory to the Lions!

King Crominus comes last, after
all the other racers. He is furious that
the noble Lions have won yet again.
That night the Crocodiles and their
allies meet to plot their revenge...

Lion patrol

The next morning, Lennox cruises around Chima in his golden Lion Attack vehicle. Lennox is a foot soldier in the Lion Tribe and he carries out daily patrols of the kingdom. He is responsible for checking that all is well.

Lennox always carries some blue CHI at the back of his truck, to power the vehicle. The CHI gives his truck's engine a super energy boost of speed and thrust.

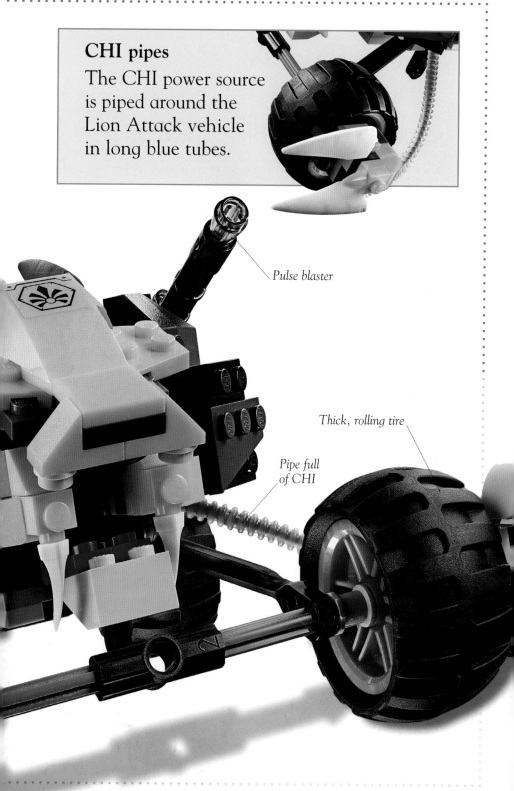

CHI pipes

The CHI power source is piped around the Lion Attack vehicle in long blue tubes.

Pulse blaster

Thick, rolling tire

Pipe full of CHI

Crafty Crocs

The power-hungry Crocodiles have hatched a rotten plan to get more CHI. They send Crug the thug to pinch the CHI from Lennox's truck as it rumbles past. Crug clumsily sneaks up next to the rear tires and grabs the CHI from its compartment.

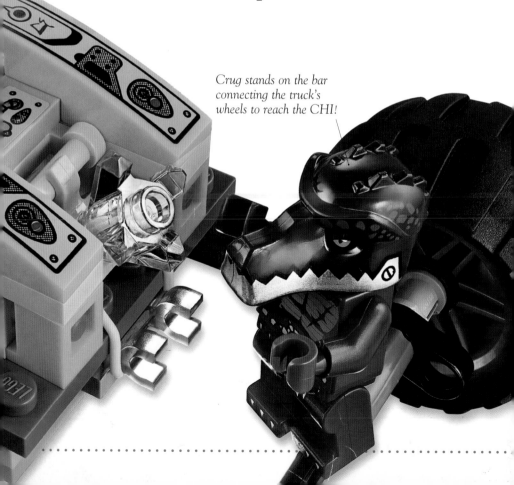

Crug stands on the bar connecting the truck's wheels to reach the CHI!

Hey! Leonidas, another Lion guard, has spotted Crug. He sprints after the scaly scoundrel, wielding his mighty sword. Pow! Crug blasts his pulse shooter back at him. It seems like Crug will escape, but at the last moment the clumsy reptile slips and takes a big fall. The CHI flies into Leonidas's outstretched paw!

Croc ambush

Leonidas is relieved to have got the CHI back. But then disaster strikes. Oh no! Those crafty Crocs have staged an ambush! Leonidas's moment of victory is short as Crawley the henchman's Claw Ripper suddenly shoots out of the undergrowth. It is traveling at top speed on its monstrously huge wheels.

The Claw Ripper grabs Leonidas and the CHI in its jaws! Crawley cackles in glee as his prisoner struggles to escape the fangs of his vicious vehicle.

Claw Ripper teeth
The piercing fangs rotate on the tracks as Crawley drives the Claw Ripper.

Poor Leonidas is still holding the CHI.

Long, lethal jaws

Showdown time

Luckily, Leonidas manages to use his silver sword to pry apart the Claw Ripper's terrible teeth. Crawley instantly leaps down from his vehicle. The sworn enemies circle the Claw Ripper, preparing to face each other on foot.

Harness holds the driver in their seat safely.

But high up
in the clouds, the
Eagles have been
watching the action
unfold on the ground.
Brave Eris is hovering above
with her golden ax. When she
sees Crawley preparing to attack
Leonidas, she swoops down to save
the precious CHI.

*Thick spikes on wheels
look like crocodile skin.*

Eagle escape!

Eris zooms back up through the sky. She quickly gets into her amazing Eagle Interceptor aircraft, with its blue wings, sharp yellow beak, and fierce flicker missiles.

Wide wingspan for gliding through the air

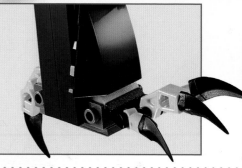

Terrifying talons
The Interceptor's feet, tipped with hooked talons, are great for landing and grabbing!

Unfortunately clever Eris has failed to notice a sneaky stowaway... and sneaking around is what the rascally Raven Tribe does best!

Greedy Razar from the Raven Tribe is an ally of the Crocodiles and has followed Eris to pilfer the CHI back. He sneaks along the back of the Interceptor and swipes the hidden CHI from its secret chest!

Razar is up to no good!

Stop thief!

Razar's sleek black Raven Glider is hovering nearby. He hops in and speeds off with the CHI!

All is not lost though—Eris is smart and has made sure that her super Eagle Interceptor is ready for emergencies. She presses the ejector button on the control panel.

Pow! The cockpit breaks away
from the body of the Interceptor. It
becomes a small, powerful jet plane.

Eris zooms after Razar and a
high-speed chase begins. She fires her
flicker missiles, which Razar quickly
dodges to avoid being hit, but he
accidentally drops his loot! Oops…

Razar moves the
glider's levers with
his handy hook!

River rapids

The precious CHI falls through the sky and lands in the river rapids below. Splash!

The Lions have been watching the battle in the skies above. Lennox and Leonidas see the CHI fall in the river and they take action.

They quickly jump onto their powerful yellow jet skis, to retrieve the Lions' CHI.

But unfortunately for them, the Crocodiles have spotted the CHI too. They board Prince Cragger's huge, scaly Command Ship. Both tribes are racing through the choppy river rapids—who will get to the CHI first?

Hurrah! The Lions reach the CHI, and Leonidas swiftly swipes it out of the choppy waters.

Prisoners in peril

The Lions are in trouble. The mighty crocodile-shaped Command Ship is right behind them. The Ship threatens the Lions with its swiping tail and enormous teeth.

The Lions are forced to surrender the CHI and board the Command Ship as prisoners. The ship's jaws snap open at the front of the boat, to reveal a spiky prison.

Cragger pokes the prisoners with his spear.

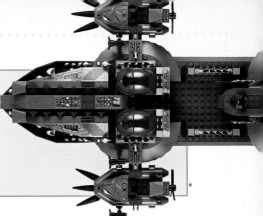

Clawsome Crocodile
Cragger's Command Ship
has terrifying, pointy claws
and two red eyes!

Prince Cragger takes the Lions'
weapons. He guards Lennox and
Leonidas with a smug crocodile smirk
on his face!

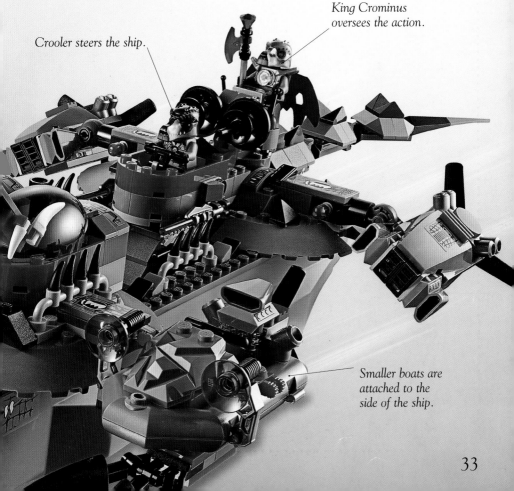

*King Crominus
oversees the action.*

Crooler steers the ship.

*Smaller boats are
attached to the
side of the ship.*

33

Scaly surprise

Leonidas has a trick up his sleeve! He crouches low and suddenly pounces on Prince Cragger. Leonidas grabs the CHI back, and his confiscated sword. King Crominus sprints over with his ferocious red and gold ax and combat breaks out!

Churning propeller blades

In the confusion, the Lions manage to fight their way free and leap over the side of the ship, into the river. They swim for the shore. Poor Lions—they hate getting their fur wet!

But crafty King Crominus also knows about surprises. The Command Ship has a Croc Helicopter attachment on the back of the boat. Crominus and Crooler jump into the aircraft and zoom off after the Lions.

Strike one

Luckily for the Lions, their help has arrived! On the river shore, mighty Equila from the Eagle Tribe appears in his fantastic Ultra Striker battle vehicle. It boasts big CHI-powered engines, churning rubber tracks, and menacing gold claws.

Just for once even those naughty Ravens might think twice about pilfering anything from this battle-ready bird!

Leonidas throws the CHI high in the air to Equila. The Eagle catches it and drives off in his Ultra Striker. The engines shriek with a piercing eagle cry.

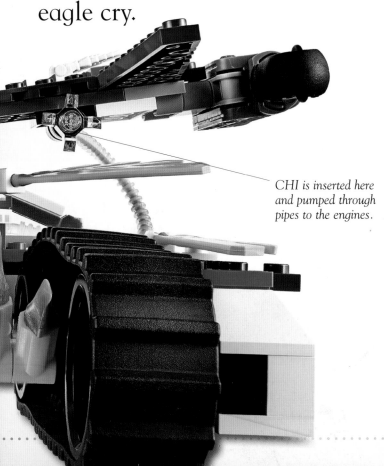

CHI *is inserted here and pumped through pipes to the engines.*

Wolf attack!

The Wolf Pack has entered the battle! Wakz of the Wolf Tribe drives a menacing Pack Tracker called an ATV (all terrain vehicle) that can travel across nearly any surface.

Wolf shooter
The Pack Tracker's gray missile launcher is topped with a Wolf Tribe flag.

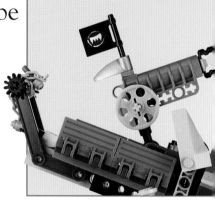

Fanged chain winch

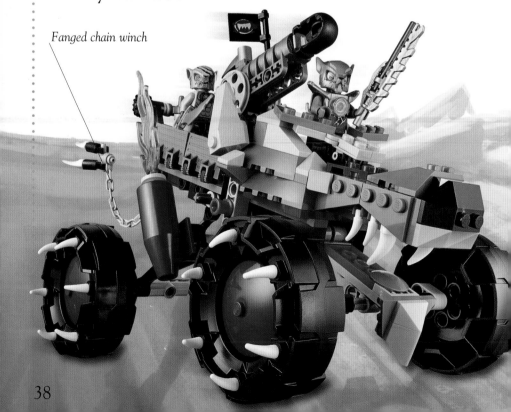

38

The Pack Tracker has spiky tires, fiery flamethrowers, and even a long fanged chain winch at the back of the vehicle. Wakz is driving while Winzar brings up the rear, aiming the missile launcher. These Wolves mean business!

As Equila flees the riverbank with the CHI in his Ultra Striker, the ruthless Wolves launch a fierce chase after him across the rocky ground.

Stealth mission

Equila gets a head start on the Wolves, and he powers away into the distance. When the Wolves are far behind and the coast is clear, the quick-thinking Eagle flicks the Ultra Striker's settings to autopilot.

Equila's golden ax is very valuable.

He then secretly climbs out of the cockpit while it's still moving!

Equila grabs the CHI and his golden ax, and jumps into the air. He flies around in a big loop so that he's back behind Wakz's Pack Tracker! Equila hopes to catch the Wolves unaware and smash the Pack Tracker's engines with his ax.

The CHI flies through the air after Equila throws it.

Fiery flamethrower

Sticky situation

Disaster strikes!
Equila flies too close
to the Pack Tracker.
Ouch! He is snared by
the fangs of the vehicle's
swinging chain winch.
The Wolves cannot believe their
luck! They start to reel in the winch.
Nasty wolfish grins spread across
their faces when they see their
captive and the CHI
getting closer.
Equila decides that if he
is about to become Wolf
breakfast, the CHI will not
share his fate. He throws
the CHI away from him and
it bounces to the jungle floor below.

Royalty to the rescue

Fast as a rocket, Crawley grabs the CHI from the floor before anyone can blink! He makes a run for it. But Prince Laval of the Lion Tribe has decided it's time to bring the chaos to an end.

Mobile map

The Royal Fighter has a handy retractable map of Chima that can be pulled out or stowed away.

Laval screeches after cheeky Crawley in his majestic Royal Fighter. He sits up in the cannon tower and fires the huge pulse blasters, while Longtooth drives the vehicle on its massive tracks.

Ferocious lion face to scare enemies

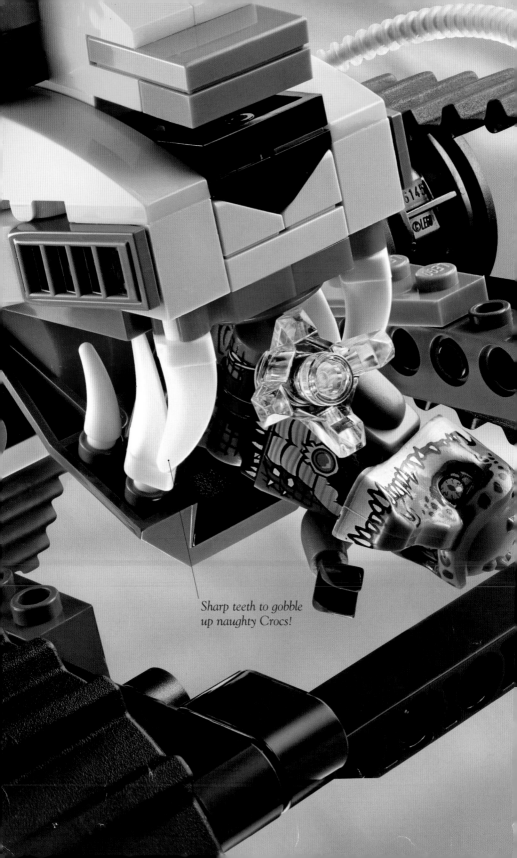

Sharp teeth to gobble up naughty Crocs!

Crocodile sandwich

Crunch! Crawley couldn't run away quickly enough! The Royal Fighter's mighty jaws have chewed him up like a tasty snack. He struggles to squeeze out of the vehicle, but the jaws are clamped too tightly.

The Lions take their prisoner on a parade around Chima for all the tribes to see. The animals howl with laughter when they spot greedy Crawley hanging upside down. He's getting a taste of his own Crocodile medicine!

Razar, Laval, Cragger, Eris, and Worriz

Poor Crawley is squirming in red-faced embarrassment. But at least the fight for CHI is over… for now!

Glossary

Agility
A person's ability to move nimbly and quickly.

Ally
A person or group who is united with another by a shared goal or aim.

Ambush
When somebody hides in wait for another person before launching a surprise attack on them.

Autopilot
A function on an aircraft that allows it to automatically follow a course set by the pilot.

Chaos
When everything is in confusion and disorder.

Chest plate
A piece of armor that protects the torso.

Competitors
People that enter and participate in a race or competition.

Confiscated
When a person's items or belongings are seized by another person.

Consequences
Results or outcome from an event, often unpleasant.

Distribute
To give out an item to others.

Epic
Grand or heroic.

Evolved
People or animals that have changed or developed gradually over time.

Flamethrower
A weapon which spits out a fiery stream of burning liquid such as gasoline.

Guardian
A person who protects and takes care of another person or thing.

Intentions
A person's desires, goals, or plans.

Majestic
Regal, magnificent, worthy of royalty.

Nerves of steel
An expression meaning lots of courage to cope in scary situations.

Orb
An object shaped like a sphere or globe.

Paradise
An idyllic place of perfection and happiness.

Patrols
To travel regularly around an area such as a kingdom to check what is happening and guard it.

Peril
Danger, being at risk.

Pilfer
To steal, especially minor or small items.

Scoundrel
A rascal or rotten person.

Smithereens
Tiny shattered pieces.

Snared
To be caught by somebody or something in a trap.

Stowaway
A person who secretly climbs on another person's vehicle before it sets off on its journey.

Swipes
Grabs or snatches.

Thug
An aggressive, violent criminal.

Tracks
The long belts that encase the wheels of heavy vehicles such as tanks. They allow the tank to move without sinking in soft ground.

Unaware
Without warning, or being caught off guard.

Undergrowth
Brambles, bushes, and short trees that grow beneath larger trees.

Index